What Animals Eat
HERBIVORES

James Benefield

raintree

Raintree is an imprint of Capstone Global Library Limited, a company incorporated in England and Wales having its registered office at 7 Pilgrim Street, London, EC4V 6LB – Registered company number: 6695582

www.raintree.co.uk
myorders@raintree.co.uk

Edited by James Benefield and Amanda Robbins
Designed by Richard Parker
Picture research by Svetlana Zhurkin
Production by Helen McCreath
Originated by Capstone Global Library Ltd
Printed and bound in China

ISBN 978 1 406 28911 4 (hardback)
18 17 16 15 14
10 9 8 7 6 5 4 3 2 1

ISBN 978 1 406 28915 2 (paperback)
19 18 17 16 15
10 9 8 7 6 5 4 3 2 1

British Library Cataloguing in Publication Data
A full catalogue record for this book is available from the British Library.

Acknowledgements
We would like to thank the following for permission to reproduce photographs:Getty Images: Manoj Shah, 12; iStockphotos: ElsvanderGun, 6; Shutterstock: Andrea Izzotti, 9, 23 (claws), Bestweb, cover, Dmitry Maslov, 7, fresie12 (pine cone), back cover, howamo, 13, Hurst Photo, 4, Jan S., 8, Jose Angel Astor Rocha, 10, Kamonrat, 14, Mohamed Zain, 11, 23 (thorn), Olesia Sarycheva, 16, 23 (grain), Pavel K (footprints), throughout, Peter Betts, 18, Raquel Pedrosa, 19, Rich Carey, 15, 23 (seagrass), Serg64, 5, Vlue (roots), back cover, 23, Willi Schmitz, 17; USDA: ARS/Keith Weller, 21.

Contents

Some words are shown in bold, **like this**.
You can find them in the glossary on page 23.

What do animals eat?

You need to eat the right food to live and grow. Animals need the right food, too. Different animals eat different things.

Herbivores eat plants. Carnivores eat meat.
Omnivores eat both meat and plants.

What is a herbivore?

Herbivores get their food from plants. Like you, they can eat fruit, vegetables, nuts and **grains**. For example, some lemurs love to eat fruit.

Some herbivores eat parts of plants that we don't usually eat. Squirrels eat tree bark and parts of **pine cones**.

How do herbivores get food?

An orangutan's long arms help it to get food. An orangutan uses its arms to swing between trees and reach for fruit.

Some herbivores find food in the ground. Wombats have sharp **claws**. These claws help them dig through soil to find **roots** to eat.

How do herbivores eat food?

Look at this horse's teeth. Many herbivores have teeth like this. Their front teeth cut up plants. Their back teeth grind plants into tiny pieces.

Some plants are hard to get at. The giraffe's long tongue can reach leaves from between sharp **thorns**.

Are herbivores predators or prey?

Animals that hunt herbivores are called predators. Animals that are hunted are called prey. Which animal is the predator in this picture?

Herbivores need to spot predators. Many herbivores, such as this deer, have eyes on the sides of their heads. They can see all around.

Herbivores all around

You can also find herbivores in the air. Blue and yellow macaw parrots eat foods such as seeds and fruit.

There are lots of herbivores in the sea.
For example, a green sea turtle eats seaweed
and **seagrasses**.

Can you find a herbivore in your home?

There are some herbivores we keep as pets. We can keep birds such as parrots or budgies. Their food includes seeds.

Rabbits are herbivores, and we can keep them as pets, too. They love to eat lettuce and vegetable scraps.

Herbivores in danger

When humans build things, they might cut down plants and trees. This happens in the Amazon rainforest. Herbivores need these plants and trees for food.

We can help herbivores in the wild by planting new trees. We can also keep some herbivores in zoos to keep them safe. For example, we can feed them the right food in zoos.

Dangerous herbivores!

Herbivores don't kill animals to eat, but they can still be dangerous. If a group of African buffalo runs towards you, you could become as flat as a pancake!

Cows are herbivores. Cows can get scared around dogs, and may run at you. Keep your pet dog on a lead when you're around cows.

True or false?

1. We call the animals that hunt herbivores their prey.

2. We eat all of the same fruit and vegetables that herbivores eat.

3. Some herbivores are in danger because humans are cutting down trees in forests.

4. We do not keep any herbivores as pets.

5. You can find herbivores on the land and in the sea, but not in the air.

6. Herbivores have grinding teeth. These teeth break down the food they eat.

6. True
5. False. Lots of birds are herbivores.
4. False. Lots of pets are herbivores.
3. True
2. False. Some herbivores like roots and pine cones.
1. False. We call them their predators.

Answers

22

Picture glossary

claw
hard, pointy and curvy end to an animal's finger or toe

grain
kind of seed, such as a grain of rice

pine cone
fruit of a pine tree. Seeds of the pine tree are inside pine cones.

root
part of a plant. It is usually below ground. It sucks up water and goodness from the soil.

seagrass
like normal grass, but lives in the sea

thorn
sharp and spiky part of some plants

Find out more

Books

Food (Why Living Things Need), Daniel Nunn
  (Raintree, 2012)
How Do Living Things Find Food? (Introducing
  Living Things), Bobbie Kalman (Crabtree, 2010)

Website

**education.nationalgeographic.com/education/
encyclopedia/herbivore/?ar_a=1**
This website has lots more about herbivores.

Index